RUSTLING LEAVES

Books by Jeremiah W. Montgomery

Soulmancer
Making Tea

ඝඝඝඝඝඝඝඝඝඝඝඝඝඝ

RUSTLING LEAVES

ඝඝඝඝඝඝඝඝඝඝඝඝඝඝ

JEREMIAH W. MONTGOMERY

WWW.PIPEANDPINT.COM
HOLLIDAYSBURG, PENNSYLVANIA

Published 2008 by Jeremiah W. Montgomery
W W W . P I P E A N D P I N T . C O M

ISBN-10: 0-9796122-3-3
ISBN-13: 978-0-9796122-3-7

Printed in the United States of America

CONTENTS

We cannot mingle with the splendours we see. But all the leaves of the New Testament are rustling with the rumour that it will not always be so.

- C.S. Lewis, *The Weight of Glory*

TO MY SONS GAVIN, LOGAN, & EWAN

PREFACE

Some time ago, I was asked to fill the pulpit for the Sunday morning service at a church in Cumberland, Maryland. Driving home alone that afternoon, I was listening to the album *Overdressed* by Caedmon's Call. The last song on that album is called, "Start Again," and as I listened I was moved by a line from the chorus which finishes with the simply cry, "I need hope to start again."

It struck me then that one of the deepest needs of humanity, one of the sweetest provisions of the Christian faith, and therefore one of the paramount needs in Christian preaching and writing – is hope.

Accordingly, I have endeavored this half-year to center my reflections upon that theme. It has not always been smooth sailing; I am inclined by nature more to the dour and melancholy. Yet in such times I am both stung and succored by the Psalmist's words:

Why are you cast down, O my soul,
and why are you in turmoil within me?
Hope in God; for I shall again praise him,
my salvation and my God.

- PSALM 42:11

There is great joy in possession of true hope. My prayer is that what follows may help, and not hinder, you in finding it. Or rather, in being found by *him*. For true hope is a not a platitude: he is a person.

In the way of acknowledgements, I confess my debt of inspiration for the title of this volume to Professor C.S. Lewis, lately of Oxford and Cambridge Universities in England. Furthermore, I should like to thank the Rev. David Douglas Gebbie of Chesley, Ontario, and a certain Donald Shumaker of Altoona, Pennsylvania, both for their friendships and their many patient hours of conversation with me on the subjects treated herein — and on numerous other things besides. Any error that remains in the words that follow is entirely my fault, but any light that may be found herein is in great part due to the wise counsel of these friends and gentlemen.

I wish to acknowledge, too, my affection and debt towards my family. My wife, my sons, my dad and mum, and my brothers — you have all helped shape me in wonderful ways which words can scarcely describe.

And lastly, to my Maker, Redeemer, and Friend: you wrote every page of my life before I was born; you give me life, breath, everything. You are my hope.

J.W.M.
Hollidaysburg, PA

DIVERSITY, DEATH, TAXES & HOPE

This week I have been travelling in southern California for business. It has been a thoroughly enjoyable few days, and God willing, I shall leave very early tomorrow morning to return home. In the meantime, this week has provided much material upon which to settle my musings.

Most of Sunday was spent in and out of airports terminals, on and off of airplanes. I finished reading one book, slept a bit, and began reading another. I overheard some interesting conversational fragments. (Really, you would be surprised what people will tell complete strangers on a long flight.) But what struck me most of all – as it always does – is the sheer diversity of the people. The larger the airport, the more variation you get. I often wonder, as I press through the human ocean of air travelers, what sort of lives must they each live? Doubtless there are common themes - employment, family, food and shelter. But, I ponder, what sort of other things concern the people passing by? What questions, if any, do they consider ultimate or of utmost importance?

As I chewed on this during one of my flights, I realized that the operation was bringing to my own attention an important question. I am a Christian. More particularly, I am one of those pesky sorts who take their faith very seriously – the kind who believe that faith in Jesus Christ is not just a good thing for me, but the only real hope for anybody. The question that

1

came to me, then, was a sort of challenge: "If your faith really is more than an existential, personal convenience – if it really is of universal scope – how do you express that?" In other words, what does Christianity have to say when faced with all this diversity of background, culture, and experience?

As a Christian, I know that there are in fact a great many things that the Scriptures have to say to the world. Things such as the reality of God and the reality of his justice. Things such as the reality of our sin and the wrath it deserves. Things such as the reality of God's great love and the Savior it has sent. Certainly all these things are important, and each has a vital place in the Christian message. The trouble is, these truths are not very simply explained or easily presented. They require context and careful explanation. That is why Scripture comes to us in 66 books rather than a five-point executive summary.

In former days, many of the common Scriptural concepts were present in the "background radiation" of Western culture. This made it somewhat easy to share the Christian message, as you could assume some knowledge of the basic points – however faint – in those with whom you conversed. As the sun sets on that era and the dark night of postmodernism approaches, however, these assumptions are no longer valid. You won't get very far telling people they need to "be right with God", if they don't understand that you are speaking of the God of Scripture rather than some distant Deist construct. Likewise with concepts such as sin and redemption. We can no longer assume a proper – or an even somewhat proper – understanding of these concepts. The grand motto of postmodernism is Pontius Pilate's famous question, "What is truth?" The question is the answer, and nothing is certain. At least, that's the idea.

The challenge this system poses to Christianity should be obvious. We can no longer begin our conversations with, "Here is absolute truth," when those with whom we speak deny the existence of absolute truth *a priori*. This is not to deny the need to bring absolute truth to bear in evangelism. That is necessary, and absolutely so. Truth is truth, and it cannot be compromised. At the same time, it is no compromise to allow the reality of our situation to inform our approach. And I think here our approach must be twofold. First, we must demonstrate that there are such things as universal truth. But second – and this is critical – we must do so without falling back on specialized terminology. If I tell a stranger I write OpenGL code in C++, their eyes will glaze over. But if I tell them I write 3D graphics like they see in video games or Pixar films, the light stays on. The same idea must be used by Christians who wish to effectively share our message.

One path I would propose, then, is as follows. It is somewhat of a cultural joke in English-speaking countries that the only two things that are certain in life are "death and taxes". This is actually quite profound, if we consider it: death and taxes, the only two certainties — the only two things that we cannot seem to avoid. Notice how both of them are negative. Nobody wants to die, and nobody likes paying taxes. But why is this? There are plenty of other things we cannot avoid that hardly excite our interest. Take, for example, gravity. If I jump up, I'll come back down. I don't get angry about this, because that's just how it is. Why then do we greet death and taxes with such venom? If they are truly unavoidable, why do we hate them so?

I think the answer is that we hate them because we sense that they should be avoidable. Somewhere deep within ourselves, we realize that both death and involuntary service (or slavery, if you like — this is what taxation is at root) are in some sense wrong; that in some way — we may not know how, exactly — they cut across the very fabric of our nature and the grain of our existence. They are certain, and yet we sense that they ought not be.

It is at this point, at this junction where postmodern mentality comes up against harsh reality, that I think the Christian message can be brought to bear. The reason we hate these things, the reason they seem contrary to our nature, says Christianity, is because they are. We were not made to die. Nor were we made to be slaves. We were made to live forever as children of God. In short, the yearnings we each experience for life and freedom are not odd fantasies or misplaced hopes. They are the very purposes for which we were made. If I may employ a computer software analogy, they are our original programming. The trouble is that this original programming has been corrupted, much like a computer which has been attacked by a virus. That virus is the reason we experience death. It is the reason slavery exists, in all its forms – from the brutal and inhumane regimes of the antebellum American (and current global) South, to the more benign systems of regulation and taxation in Western democracies.

You can call this virus 'evil' if you like, or you can use the biblical word, 'sin'. What we name it is not terribly important. What is important is that we recognize it as the root of all things wrong, in both ourselves and in the world. It is a corruption that affects us at all levels of our being. It affects our hearts, our minds, and even our bodies. It is the reason we hate, and it is the reason we perpetuate that hatred through inhumane actions. It is the reason we die, and it is the reason we make slaves. In fact, it itself is the thing which enslaves us most. In short, sin/evil is the reason for both death and taxes.

It is when we come to terms with this universal experience of death, taxes, and the evil which lies in back of them both, that we find ourselves in a position to answer my original question. What does Christianity have to say in the face of all the diversity of background, culture, and experience in the world? It says three things. The first thing it says is that there are experiences common to all humanity. The second thing it says is that these experiences point us to some absolute truths about ourselves. In other words, these first two steps do just what we've already done in discussing death and taxes — they point to the universal experiences and they explain why they are, in fact, universal. It is only after we have done this that Christianity is able to say the third and greatest thing.

Christianity does not merely point out the problems with the world, as though we were all really too dense to notice them for ourselves. It is not a harping faith; rather, it is a heralding faith. And what is it that Christianity heralds? Hope.

The essence of the message of Christianity — the essence of its Gospel ("good news") — is that there is a cure for evil, a cure for death & slavery to sin. Now of course Christianity is not the only religion out there that claims to know such a cure, is it? Why then should it be preferred over other religions? What makes its claims unique, its purported hope any more hopeful?

The difference between Christianity and all other religions is the source of its hope. To varying degrees or another, all other religions in the world place the source of hope upon humanity itself. According to these religions, deliverance from evil is at least partly up to human efforts. What makes Christianity unique is that we say — kindly, but firmly — that this idea is rubbish. If what we have discussed above is correct, if the virus of evil really does infect humans as well as everything else, then the idea of deliverance from evil being up to humans — even in part – is akin to allowing the inmates to administer the asylum, or setting a kleptomaniac to watch the store.

The unique claim of Christianity is that deliverance can only come – and in fact has come – from outside of humanity. This is why we are so insistent that Jesus Christ was not merely a man, but also God himself. If he were just a man, then he's got the same problems we do, and we are all just going round in circles. But if he is in fact God (as we confess he is), then there is real hope of deliverance – real hope that the cycle of evil was broken by one who was not infected by it. This is precisely the Christian message: that God himself became a sinless man, by whose death the penalty for evil is paid, and by whose life and resurrection the victory over death and slavery was secured. What humanity cannot do, God has done – and all those who put their trust in Jesus Christ will thereby receive the benefits of his accomplishment: payment of the penalty for their sins, liberation from slavery to evil, and a share in Jesus' resurrection to everlasting life.

So what does Christianity offer to the world? Amidst all the diversity, death and taxes in the world – this is what we hold and share: Hope. Real hope. And unlike all other religions or self-help systems, the hope that is in us does not rest – even in the smallest bit – upon our efforts. Even the faith which unites us to Jesus is a gift from God. It does not work; it only trusts. And for this reason – because it rests wholly upon God and not in the least upon humanity – the hope of Christianity is strong and sure.

Diversity, death, and taxes. But hope. Hope!

January 17, 2008

THE DAYS ARE COMING

William Wordsworth once wrote a sonnet whose title and opening line were, "the world is too much with us." At some point during my twenty-seven years in this life, that single line found its way into my mind. I cannot recall when this happened. In fact, as I sat down to write this I was sure I was remembering a line from Shakespeare – and it was only when I searched for the exact reference that I found the author to be not the Bard, but a Romantic. Go figure.

Regardless of how or when (or even whence) the line came, it has always stuck with me. Many times over the years I have found it echoing in my thoughts. Not with the clear, ringing peals of Scripture. The words do not resound like bell-song across a verdant quad. No indeed, they float more like overheard snatches of a whisper along a cool, dark corridor. If the promised hopes of Scripture are the songs of Spring, then these words of Wordsworth are the haunting lament of (the) Fall.

A few months ago, I came across the following passage in the book of the Old Testament prophet Amos:

In that day I will raise up the booth of David that is fallen and repair its breaches, and raise up its ruins and rebuild it as in the days of old...

"Behold, the days are coming," declares the LORD, "when the plowman shall overtake the reaper and the treader of grapes him who sows the seed; the mountains shall drip sweet wine, and all the hills shall flow with it. I will restore the fortunes of my people Israel, and they shall rebuild the ruined cities and inhabit them; they shall plant vineyards and drink their wine, and they shall make gardens and eat their fruit. I will plant them on their land, and they shall never again be uprooted out of the land that I have given them," says the LORD your God.[1]

What struck about this passage as I read it is the vividness of the hope it portrays. So often we are so burdened with our reaping and sowing – our daily work and toil – that we forget that it does not last forever. Sometimes the corridors in which we walk are so long and dark that we forget, or fail to see, the light of day shining through the window at the end. This passage reminds us, though, that there is an end of toil and trouble. "The days are coming," it declaims – and what glorious days! A bountiful harvest approaches. There will be so many grapes to tread that the very mountains will drip with sweet wine!

The fortunes of God's people will be restored. Cities will be rebuilt; vineyards and gardens will be planted. And not only will they be planted, but those

---

[1] Amos 9:11, 13-15

who do the planting will enjoy their produce. The imagery here is carefully chosen to convey a sense of permanence: gardens take months, wine making stretches beyond the growing cycle, and cities take years to rebuild. The restoration that is coming is coming forever. "I will plant them on their land, and they shall never again be uprooted..." There's a glorious finality to those words — a joyous, restful rootedness.

The world is too much with us. But the days are coming when it shall not be thus! Can we imagine such a world — such a *Paradise Restored*? There is beautiful imagery that describes this restoration world in the very last book of Scripture:

> Then I saw a new heaven and a new earth, for the first heaven and the first earth had passed away, and the sea was no more. And I saw the holy city, new Jerusalem, coming down out of heaven from God, prepared as a bride adorned for her husband. And I heard a loud voice from the throne saying, "Behold, the dwelling place of God is with man. He will dwell with them, and they will be his people, and God himself will be with them as their God. He will wipe away every tear from their eyes, and death shall be no more, neither shall there be mourning, nor crying, nor pain anymore, for the former things have passed away."

And he who was seated on the throne said, "Behold, I am making all things new." Also he said, "Write this down, for these words are trustworthy and true." And he said to me, "It is done! I am the Alpha and the Omega, the beginning and the end. To the thirsty I will give from the spring of the water of life without payment. The one who conquers will have this heritage, and I will be his God and he will be my son. But as for the cowardly, the faithless, the detestable, as for murderers, the sexually immoral, sorcerers, idolaters, and all liars, their portion will be in the lake that burns with fire and sulfur, which is the second death."[2]

A world without crying or pain. A world without death. A world where all wrongs are put to right. It all sounds so great, so promising – that is, until we reach the last verse. As we start looking through the list of those excluded, we start to cringe. We may not have murdered or practiced sorcery. But have we ever been sexually immoral? Have we ever lied? Have we ever acted the coward? If so, where does this leave us? Is all this stuff about a restoration simply piling-on, just a picture-postcard meant to torture the prisoners? "Look at this lovely place – too bad you'll never see it!" Is that really how it goes? Is God being sadistic? Or perhaps (more likely, some would say), is it all just too good to

---

[2] Revelation 21:1-8

be true: "pie in the sky, heaven when you die"; meanwhile buck-up and wallow in the sty?

The answer to these questions is, of course, "No." God is no sadist, nor is the promised restoration a pile-on or merely pie in the sky. We are all guilty and undeserving sinners. If we have no hope but ourselves, then we are indeed damned – and damnably so – for there can be no guilt or sin in the world to come. But thank God, there is a hope extended that comes to us from outside ourselves – a hope that our sins can be paid for and ourselves cleansed. You see, I am not the first person to try to apply the words of the prophet Amos to our contemporary situation. The apostles Peter and James did so nearly two thousand years ago, when they said:

> But we believe that we will be saved through the grace of the Lord Jesus, just as they will... And with this the words of the prophets agree, just as it is written, "After this I will return, and I will rebuild the tent of David that has fallen; I will rebuild its ruins, and I will restore it, that the remnant of mankind may seek the Lord, and all the Gentiles who are called by my name, says the Lord, who makes these things known from of old."[3]

---

[3] Acts 15:11, 15-18

Quoting the words of Amos the prophet and making allusion to the language of a handful of other prophets, the apostles tie all the promises of restoration to a single hope: the grace of the Lord Jesus.

In the time of the New Testament, Israel was ruled by Roman overlords. The line of kings descended from David had fallen. In Jesus Christ – whose human ancestry traced back to David – the once-and-future kingdom of David is restored. But this kingdom was not restored to rule a narrow tract of land in Palestine. Jesus came to provide to a remnant of mankind the way to seek God. God himself became man in order to make man right with God – in order to provide a gate of entrance into that *Paradise Restored* whose days are coming. Not all mankind will enter by that gate. Many will be lost. But a remnant will enter. A remnant will be saved by the grace of the Lord Jesus.

And this is the crux of the whole matter. The days are coming. A new earth and new heavens are on their way. The only way to enter is by the grace of the Lord Jesus Christ, and the only way to receive that grace is through faith alone. John Murray described faith as self-abandonment to Christ. That puts the point on it precisely. We cannot enter the new world by our own efforts. We are corrupt and guilty, and we need to be cleansed. Unless the filthy rags of our sins are exchanged for the clean garments of Christ's imputed righteousness, we cannot attend the feast. This necessary exchange is made through faith alone. It is for this reason – because we are fully foul and only

Christ is completely clean – that any attempt to augment or circumvent the finished work of Christ tramples grace and damns the race. Entrance to *Paradise Restored* comes only to those who abandon themselves to Jesus the Lord.

The world is too much with us. Can we imagine it otherwise? Dare we have such a hope? If we abandon ourselves to Christ, we don't have to scratch our heads and wonder. The answers are, "Yes and yes – a thousand times yes!" In him we have hope of a joy and peace and permanence that will never be uprooted. Never! In him we will plant gardens and eat their produce. In him we will plant vineyards and drink their wine. In him we will rebuild the ruined cities and inhabit them. From him – and him alone – we who thirst may and will receive from the spring of the water of life without payment. It is in this hope – with this glorious end in sight – that we find strength to carry on today.

The long night of the world is grim. The darkness is heavy, and it weighs us down. But dawn will not tarry forever. The days are coming!

February 19, 2008

15

The Well-Digger

Imagine if you will a beautiful country, a verdant land of hill and dale, of cool thick forests and long running rivers. Imagine the chimes of birdsong in every bush, and the feel of the warm breeze rustling through the grass and caressing your face. Imagine the cycles of such a dreamscape: dawn and dusk, milk and honey. The sun rises with healing it its wings, and it sets with rest in its wake. There is justice in every hall, and peace upon each leaf. There is milk in every child's cup, and honey in each comb and on each table.

Then imagine drought coming to this country. Vivid green becomes dull brown. Leaves curl, foliage die; the once-flowing rivers all run dry. The sun scorches in the morning, and the wind moans at dusk like the last rattling breath from a dying husk. Children cry for nourishment, and there is none. Honey-pots are broken – for they have no other use.

Drought comes to all people. Believer or unbeliever, Christian or not – we've all experienced the inner scorching of an invisible sun: hot, merciless, withering our souls with every ray. The pain of spiritual dryness is common to all people, and even the most faithful Christians are not immune. Why does this happen? How should we deal with it? In my experience, there are chiefly five causes. Since four of these pertain to Christians, let us consider them first.

In many cases, drought is a result of ignorance or forgetfulness. A Christian is one who knows he can only be right with God through the life, death, and resurrection of Christ, who has been given this gift of faith by God's grace, and who therefore trusts Christ alone to make him right with God. This trust encompasses not only the forgiveness of our sins, but also our need for positive righteousness before our holy Creator. This sense of what it means to be a Christian is captured by three of the great *solas* of the Reformation: *sola gratia*, *sola fide*, and *solus Christus*: by grace alone, through faith alone, in Christ alone. The leaders of the Reformation rightly insisted that the one article by which the Christian Church stands or falls is justification by faith alone. We who are Christians are such – and remain such from our conversions into eternity – by grace through faith in Christ alone. Period.

Some Christians, however, do not understand this. Perhaps they were never taught it. There are many so-called churches that teach people that right standing with God is based – in part or in whole – upon our own efforts or upon our decision. I'm sure we've all heard this before, especially at funerals: "Bob was a good and kind man; we just *know* he's in heaven." The emphasis in such statements always hides the uncertainty, though: *how good is good enough? Did Bob really make it?*

On the other hand, perhaps we have been taught correctly the grace-centered nature of Christian faith – but have forgotten or gotten confused. You see, the fruit of true Christian faith is evangelical obedience: Christians are commanded to love the Lord with all their heart, soul, strength, and mind – and to love their neighbors as themselves. This obedience does not constitute our faith – it is the proof that God has constituted faith in us. When we are not careful to maintain this distinction, however, it is easy to get confused. We started to mistake the fruit with the root. We start to see good works not as the cheerful, loving response to God's grace – but as some sort of mortgage payment we make on our salvation. The result this has is catastrophic. By changing grace into duty – by damming up the river to make a reservoir, when it ought to have flown freely – we create deserts in our souls.

While we are on the subject of evangelical obedience, it's important also to remember that sometimes we don't. No Christian is ever free of sin in this life, and oft-times the failure to love God and/or our neighbor has dramatic consequences – whether this failure is ours directly or in those close to us. During the reign of King Ahab in the Old Testament, God sent a drought on Israel for three years. Did every Israelite participate directly in the idolatries of Ahab and Jezebel? Nope; but disobedience has consequences that often spread beyond the individuals involved.

All of this said, sometimes there is simply no obvious reason (so far as we can discern) for a period of spiritual dryness. In such cases, we should remember three things. Firstly, that even though we humans be the highest of creatures, we are creatures nonetheless – and therefore subject to all the passions that come with flesh. Sometimes spiritual drought is not due so much to disobedience as it is to bad digestion or a poor night's sleep. The second thing to remember is that God will sometimes use these occasions to remind us that our faith is *not* rooted in our subjective, day-to-day or momentary experience – but in the accomplished, finished work of Jesus Christ. And there are no Christians who have come so far that we no longer need such reminders. Sometimes, then, drought is like vegetables: believe it or not, it's good for you! Lastly, in such circumstances we need to remember that even when we feel very far from God, he is not far from us or lacking in power. God never ceases to be both omnipresent and omnipotent. I will return to this shortly.

The last cause of spiritual drought occurs among unbelievers – those who are not of the faith of Christ. Its cause is perhaps the simplest of all to discern, though the most difficult of all to cure. The cause is unbelief. As I have alluded to in another place, "the world is too much with us." Without hope in Christ that a day of deliverance is coming, there is simply no salve for this throbbing pain, this ache of death and decay that surrounds us. As the Book of Common Prayer puts it, "even in life we are in the midst of death." And if you have no hope in the one who was raised from the dead – and who promises to raise his own people from death into life – then even the greenest landscape holds a tinge of terror. *It will fade eventually. Entropy prevails, everything dies – and then what? Nothingness, if we're lucky – worse if we're not.*

Whatever the cause spiritual drought in our lives, there is only one cure. For both Christians and unbelievers, the only hope of restoration lies in the sovereign grace of God. If we have lost sight of this grace, if we have perverted it into duty, or if we have failed to love God in response to his grace – we must remember one thing: that the grace is not contingent upon the obedience of man. It comes as free gift, and it is always available to those who confess their sins and turn again (perhaps again and again) in faith to Christ.

Alternatively, if we can discern no cause in ourselves for the drought, then it remains for us to wait on the Lord. We must fix in our minds the conviction that God never fully or finally abandons his children, or allows them to fall away. The faith in Christ we have been given is like a well, dug deep in our souls by the gracious and strong hands of the Almighty Well-Digger. At times he may let the well run low – so low, in fact, that all we have left is dry walls and mud at the bottom. But we must remember: God never digs a well he does not intend to fill.

Lastly, for those who realize that the cause of their drought is unbelief: if you know this is the case and wish it were not so, then I urge you – look to Christ. Cast yourself upon his mercy, look to him and be saved. None who put their faith in him will be lost. None who trust in him will be ashamed. God never forsakes the soul in whom he digs a vessel of faith. With the Well-Digger there is hope: for he never digs a well he will not fill.

March 11, 2008

CONVERSION ANXIETY

Christians are commanded not to be anxious. The Lord Jesus said as much in one of the most well-known discourses in the New Testament, the Sermon on the Mount:

Therefore I tell you, do not be anxious about your life, what you will eat or what you will drink, nor about your body, what you will put on. Is not life more than food, and the body more than clothing? Look at the birds of the air: they neither sow nor reap nor gather into barns, and yet your heavenly Father feeds them. Are you not of more value than they? And which of you by being anxious can add a single hour to his span of life? And why are you anxious about clothing? Consider the lilies of the field, how they grow: they neither toil nor spin, yet I tell you, even Solomon in all his glory was not arrayed like one of these. But if God so clothes the grass of the field, which today is alive and tomorrow is thrown into the oven, will he not much more clothe you, O you of little faith? Therefore do not be anxious, saying, 'What shall we eat?' or 'What shall we drink?' or 'What shall we wear?' For the Gentiles seek after all these things, and your heavenly Father knows that you need them all. But seek first the kingdom of God and his righteousness, and all these things will be added to you.[4]

We are not to worry about what we shall eat or what we shall drink. If we are faithful and obedient in seeking God's kingdom, God will provide our needs. Worrying about it, Jesus says, won't do a rum thing. This is something we all need to be reminded of from time to time.

However, there is another thing that Christians – especially us pesky evangelical sorts – do worry about. In fact, we seem even to count it a virtue of sorts. The thing to which I am referring is the conversion of our friends and family. (Curiously, we seem to expend much less emotional energy over the conversion of our enemies... but I digress.) In this we are positively faithful in our frettings and fritterings. "Oh, I do worry about Bob... what if he never comes to know Jesus?"

Now I am not poking fun here. If dear old Bob never comes to know Jesus, then he will spend eternity in Hell. (Yes, *really*.) That is far, far from a joking matter. Moreover, I myself have many friends and family members for whose conversion I hope and pray. (You know who you are.) The point, friends, is that the same things Jesus said in regard to food and clothing also apply here. Which of us, by being anxious, can change a heart? How much fretting does it take to save

---

[4] Matthew 6:25-33

a soul? We are accustomed to thinking that it is some great act of piety to wrap ourselves around the axle over these things. But is it?

Let's take a look at another passage of Scripture. The parable of the growing seed relates directly to the spread and growth of the kingdom of God – viz., conversions:

> And he said, "The kingdom of God is as if a man should scatter seed on the ground. He sleeps and rises night and day, and the seed sprouts and grows; he knows not how. The earth produces by itself, first the blade, then the ear, then the full grain in the ear. But when the grain is ripe, at once he puts in the sickle, because the harvest has come."[5]

We can learn three things from this parable. Firstly, that sowing the seed of the kingdom of God is a real job that requires real work. The seed of the kingdom is the Word of God – the infallible, written Scriptures of the Old and New Testaments. Sowing it is the work of evangelism – sharing, teaching, but especially preaching the Bible. Sharing and teaching evangelism takes many forms: books, conversations, tracts (yes, even tracts), and sometimes even the unguided solitary reading of the Scriptures.

---

[5] Mark 4:26-29

These are all quite good, insofar as they are done faithfully, and God has used all of them as means of quickening faith in the hearts of unbelievers. Nothing, however, can replace the preaching of Scripture as the singularly most effective form of evangelism. Any evangelistic attempt that stops short of inviting a person to come hear the Word preached is truncated at best - and a betrayal at worst. In sum, then, the first lesson of the parables is that conversions don't happen without active evangelism on the part of the church and individual believers.

The second lesson from this text is one we have to infer. Although our text does not say so explicitly, we can well assume that the farmer who has so laboriously sown the seed in his field is going to pray for God's blessing on his efforts. Just so with the work of evangelism. Christians are commanded to pray for both the evangelists and those evangelized. So it is neither wrong nor inappropriate to pray for both our ministers and our lost friends and family. In fact, to neglect to do so is sin on the part of Christians.

The last lesson we are to learn from this text is that even the best farmer cannot turn seeds into grain. He might take the greatest of care in sowing, and he might pray fervently for the Lord's blessing upon his work. But in the end, the results are not up to him. As my own minister once put it in a title of a sermon: God gives the growth.

And it is for this reason that 'conversion anxiety' is as useless as food or clothing anxiety. Just as we have no power in ourselves to add an hour to our lives or guarantee our next meal, so we have no power to convert an unbeliever. If we live, if we eat – it is by the grace of God. If we have crossed from death to life through saving faith in Jesus Christ, it is likewise purely due to the grace of God.

So let's do all we can to sow the kingdom of God. Let's share the Word of God with our friends, family, and even our enemies. Let's share with them the love of Christ in word and deed, and let's invite them to church. Let's support our churches and ministers through prayers and cheerful offerings. Let's pray fervently for God to grow saving faith and spread his kingdom in our hearts, in our families, in our churches, in our communities, and around the world. All of this is part and parcel of the Great Commission – it's part of what being a Christian means.

But let us not worry about the results. They aren't ours to control. Nobody ever lengthened his life by worrying. Likewise, worry never saved a soul.

March 12, 2008

I've been thinking a lot the last day or so about the place of irenics vs. polemics in Christian conversation. The word 'irenic' means conciliatory, and comes from the Greek word for 'peace'. 'Polemic' derives from the Greek for 'hostile' or 'warlike', and is used to describe aggressive, disputatious behavior – or a person engaged in the same.

The Scriptures seem to be of almost two minds on the subject, depending on where you look:

> We destroy arguments and every lofty opinion raised against the knowledge of God, and take every thought captive to obey Christ[6]

> As for the one who is weak in faith, welcome him, but not to quarrel over opinions.[7]

> Who is wise and understanding among you? By his good conduct let him show his works in the meekness of wisdom. But if you have bitter jealousy and selfish ambition in your hearts, do not boast and be false to the truth. This is not the wisdom that comes down from above, but is earthly, unspiritual, demonic. For where jealousy and selfish ambition exist, there will be

---

[6] 2 Corinthians 10:5
[7] Romans 14:1

disorder and every vile practice. But the wisdom from above is first pure, then peaceable, gentle, open to reason, full of mercy and good fruits, impartial and sincere. And a harvest of righteousness is sown in peace by those who make peace.[8]

These are but a few citations. The book of Acts is full of more narrative accounts: Apollos publicly and powerfully refuted in Ephesus, while Paul's apologetic in Athens was more philosophical in its tone.

What is to be made of this? Some folks behave as though they only believe the first passage cited. These are the self-appointed polemicists and watchdog[ma]s of the church today. They labor to fine-tune their ears, "the better to find error, my sweet!" These folks like to think they are doing God's work by tearing down every person who puts one foot wrong, and if you dare (yes, *dare*) to question them, they will clobber you over the head with the first verse cited above – usually in an uncivil tone, and with plenty of negative implications about your faith to boot.

How do I know all this? Well, the old saying is true: it takes one to know one. As I've alluded to elsewhere, I used to be quite the polemicist. I use to give grief not only to fellow layman in the church, but even to my former pastor. So if you're reading this and feel like I'm targeting you, please remember: I've been

---

[8] James 3:13-18

there myself, and sometimes even now find myself drifting back in that direction.

The second Scripture cited above not only tells us how we should deal with polemicists – it also tells us a bit about why they are who they are. That reason is weakness of faith. Now again, I can smell the smoke coming from some of my readers' ears. "How dare you impugn my faith, you little…?" Once again, however, the truth is that I know this from experience. The worst years of my polemicism were also the years when, deep down, I was weakest in my faith. I didn't really understand grace back then, and so was insecure and unassured of my salvation. Though I never did so consciously, I tried to compensate – I tried to find my missing assurance – in my own understanding. But because I was insecure in this regard, I repeatedly had to prove to myself the greatness of my own understanding by trotting it out and clobbering people with it. Angry young Calvinist? You bet. And so (no surprise), the Scripture was vindicated: I was a disputer because I was a weakling.

Several things came together over recent years to turn me around. For starters, I myself was accused of embracing heresy. Let me tell you, friends, there is little better way to internalize the destructive power of a gun than to have a loaded one pointed in your direction. But secondly and more importantly, about a year ago God taught me what grace was really about. And that changed everything.

Which brings us to the third cited Scripture. It's no mistake that the first adjectives attributed to godly wisdom are 'meekness' and 'pure'. The Christian message is an exclusive message: that salvation & resurrection only come through faith in Christ. However, it is because of the nature of this faith – because it is a gift of God, not contingent upon anything we do – that all the other adjectives are appended: "peaceable, gentle, open to reason, full of mercy and good fruits, impartial and sincere". The Christian religion is a religion of grace; it only makes sense, then, that Christian wisdom must be gracious.

This doesn't mean that Christians should never refute error. When the need arises, we should. What it does preclude, however, is a critical, polemical attitude in how we conduct ourselves. Blowhard attitudes and behavior have no place in the life of a Christian or in the ministry of the church. This is something over which I have found myself – and still do on occasion, though by God's grace it's less often – in need of repentance.

One of the ways to avoid falling into this temptation is to simply ask ourselves when conducting our conversation: why am I doing this? If the answer is anything less (or more) than out of a sense of grace and love – anything other than love for the other person and a desire to share the grace we've received - then we must not proceed. Where jealously and selfish ambition dwell (this applies to those of us with a pathological desire to prove ourselves correct), there is only disorder and vileness.   But a harvest of righteousness only comes by peacemakers sowing peace.

March 18, 2008

CONFESSION OF A RECOVERING ARMINIAN

Christianity is the religion of grace. As a Christian, graciousness is perhaps the part of God's character in which I take most solace. As a sinner, however, grace is also one of the most difficult things for me to accept. I've written on this previously.

This afternoon I spent about an hour lying in the grass under a big old tree in a nearby park. I'm particularly fond of the park in question because it is so quiet; I'm particularly fond of the tree in question because it is so gnarled. I went to the park to spend some time pondering the relationship of grace to faith. I was somewhat torn as to whether or not this is a good idea.

To the extent that I know myself, I know that I have a tendency to over-think things. Just last night I realized that, to a very large extent, this proclivity to over-think is the source of much of my restlessness in regards to Christian assurance. I have been defining assurance of salvation in terms of my understanding: specifically, in my ability to answer all of my own theological questions. In times when I can't think of any questions to stump myself, I feel assured. But any time a question comes along to which I do not know the answer, my little house of cards collapses – and I'm left there whining that I have to start all over.

The problem with this approach should be glaring: I am resting in myself, not in Christ. For a Christian, that is a huge no-no. And I know it. Having recognized and repented of this sin some time ago, I thought that I was over it. Alas! Were it only so! I feel kind of like a relapsed alcoholic – a guy who, having gone through one rehab session, thinks he's able now to return to hanging out in the pub. This is exactly what it is like for me. Having gotten over trusting in my understanding once – over a year ago – I thought I was clean & cured for good. As it turns out, however, that is not the case: spiritual sobriety, like temperance, is a process – not a switch.

Anyway, this is why I was torn as to whether or not it was a good idea to go to the park today. Suppose that, in all my musings of faith and grace, that I were to arrive at some helpful conclusions. Would that really help me, or would it just reinforce my bad habit of trusting my synapses instead of my Savior? On the other hand, what if the Lord were to lead me to figure out something that really could help point me away from myself? That was my dilemma. So I went to the park to ponder.

For awhile, all my thinking was noise. I prayed to the Lord, explaining my frustrations and asking for his help. I percolated over a passage from one of Paul's letters:

But God, being rich in mercy, because of the great love with which he loved us, even when we were dead in our trespasses, made us alive together with Christ—by grace you have been saved— and raised us up with him and seated us with him in the heavenly places in Christ Jesus, so that in the coming ages he might show the immeasurable riches of his grace in kindness toward us in Christ Jesus. For by grace you have been saved through faith. And this is not your own doing; it is the gift of God, not a result of works, so that no one may boast.[9]

I had gone to this passage last night before bed. I went back to it this afternoon in order to see if it might help unravel my issue.

My issue goes like this: I believe that Scripture teaches salvation is by grace alone, through faith alone (not by works), and that faith is a gift of God. And yet, faith is still something we do – we believe in, we trust, the Lord Jesus. In that case, is it possible that we could be trusting Jesus as Lord and Savior the wrong way, and so not be saved?

It came to me then, however, that there are two problems with this question. The first goes thus: if faith is a gift of God, yet possible to be done wrong, then God is handing out defective gifts. The thought of this shook me. I would never intentionally accuse God of peddling bad merchandise; nevertheless, if my question were answered in the affirmative, that is exactly what I would be doing.

The second problem was more profound yet. As a Calvinist, and I admit that faith is a gift of God.

---

[9] Ephesians 2:4-9

And yet, if I allow that this gift can be wrongly (and ineffectively) used, what I am really doing is changing this gift from the instrument of salvation into the basis of salvation. If salvation depends on me taking God's gift of faith and using in the right way, then salvation is no longer something I receive entirely as a gift – it's something I earn partly. In other words, what my question was suggesting was not Calvinism, but Arminianism.

Now I love my Arminian brothers in Christ. However, I do not wish to join them – mainly because I don't trust myself to even *partly* earn *anything*. When it became clear to me that this is where my question was leading, I realized I had taken a wrong turn. Ephesians 2:8 says that we are saved *through* faith – not *because* of it. And in the very next verse it says that this salvation through faith is a gift of God – not a result of works.

I think it was right around this point that a simple – yet important – distinction came to the forefront of my thinking. *Christ does not choose to save us because we believe; we believe because he chose to save us.* It seems to me that this statement unpacks the passage in Ephesians in two important ways. Firstly, it emphasizes grace as the sole basis of salvation. But secondly – and more to the point, in light of my primary concern – it excludes the idea that faith contributes anything to that grace. This gave me the answer to my main question.

Is it possible that we could be trusting Jesus as Lord and Savior the wrong way, and so not be saved? No. The reason that this is impossible is that our trusting Jesus contributes nothing to the basis for our salvation. The sole basis for our salvation is Christ's finished work. When God saves us, he doesn't apply that finished work in half-measures. God does not give us eyes to see, and then take his hands off to see where we'll look: he gives us eyes to see, and then turns those eyes to Christ. And from the moment we see Christ, we are saved. Nowhere in this chain is a contingency upon our actions introduced. Why not? Because it is by grace we are saved through faith. Not by our own doing, not a result of our works. It's the gift of God. Christ does not choose to save us because we believe; we believe because he has chosen to save us.

This is the conclusion with which I left the park this afternoon. It seemed to me a helpful one, and so I left optimistic. However, I was not terribly comfortable holding this conclusion without some sort of expert support. So when I came home from worship this evening, I dug around a bit in my books, where I found the following quotations to support my conclusion:

> If salvation at any point is contingent upon some contribution which man himself makes, then at that point it is *of ourselves*, and to that extent it is not of grace. Paul's definition 'and

that not of yourselves' is thereby effaced and the true nature of grace is denied.[10]

Here we have the same principle exemplified and confirmed: grace knows no human contribution. If of grace, then it is wholly and exclusively of grace. Since salvation is of grace, it is all of grace.[11]

Did I learn something today? I think so. Will this enhanced understanding of grace humble me to rest wholly in Christ, or will it only reinforce my tendency to rest on my understanding? I fear the latter, but I pray for the former. One of these days, I really am going to have to stop whining and just trust Jesus. I hope – and I pray – that such a day has begun.

April 28, 2008

ON REFLECTION: Almost exactly one month after penning this, I was sitting in a hotel room in southern California, reading a book and preparing to quit my job, when I came across another quotation on the same subject. It's so good that I had to include it here. On the question of what would happen if we had to gin up a

---

[10] John Murray, <u>Collected Writings of John Murray</u> (Edinburgh: Banner of Truth Trust, 1976) Vol. 1, p. 120.
[11] Ibid., p. 122

certain level or quality of faith in Christ in order to be saved, Tim Keller writes:

> Working on the quality and purity of your commitment would become a way to merit salvation and put God in your debt. It is not the depth and purity of your heart but the work of Jesus Christ on our behalf that saves us.[12]

I thank God for Tim's clarity. Let the recovery continue!

---

[12] Timothy Keller, <u>The Reason for God: Belief in an Age of Skepticism</u> (New York: Penguin, 2008), p. 234.

A SENSE OF PRESENCE

Two winters ago, I had the opportunity to attend a reception in the gallery of the Library of Congress in Washington, D.C. In his welcoming remarks, the reception's host pointed out that the Library had a "sense of presence." The articulation was perfect; for indeed, the gallery of the Library of Congress is one of the most beautiful and stunning interiors that I have ever seen. Ever since that night, the phrase has stuck with me.

I was reminded of this phrase this morning, when I attended the memorial service for the mother of a friend. "Memorial service" is too meager a term; the better name was the one printed on the bulletin: "service of resurrection". Perhaps in practical terms they amount to same thing; yet there is in the latter a potent emphasis lacking in the former.

The service of resurrection was held at St. Stephen's Episcopal Church in Sewickley, Pennsylvania. Sewickley is an old, wealthy suburb of Pittsburgh situated about a dozen miles northwest of the city along the Ohio River. I'm not sure how old St. Stephen's Church is; the grandeur of the architecture (or its 'impracticality', as our impoverished modern sensibilities would refer to it) seemed to indicate that the parish is nearly as old as the town, which if accurate would date it to more than a century.

More interesting than its age, however, is the parish's vibrancy. When I expressed some surprise at the size of the facilities, I was told that St. Stephen's has over 2500 members! More important than the bare numbers, however, is the thing around which they all have gathered: and that is the Gospel. That this church is centered on the Lord Jesus Christ was evident everywhere – in its literature, in the spirit of the parishioners, and in the minister's homily.

Which brings me around to the sense of presence. Now I know that all of the world is God's world, and that everything in it belongs to him. I realize that true worshippers of Christ worship him in spirit and in truth, not with whitewashed sepulchres. Nevertheless, there was a definite sense of presence in St. Stephen's Church this morning.

How can I describe the experience? Upon entering, one is almost immediately struck by the sheer scale of the sanctuary, the span of its enormous rafters, and the intricate details of the stained-glass and the wood trim. It was impressed upon me just how much bigger is Christ and his Church than I. Now to be sure, this was not the first time I had contemplated this truth. But too often in life, I am like a man who looks at himself in a mirror, only to go away forgetting what I look like. That is to say, I forget how truly small I am – especially before God. Today I was humbled. The experience was not unkind, however; just a gentle reminder.

The service of resurrection itself was beautiful. The opening hymn – "I Sing a Song of the Saints of God" – was majestic in its music, yet utterly earthy (in a good way) in its lyrics. I don't know if my friend hand-picked this song himself, or whether it was requested by his mother before her death. Regardless, it set the tone for all that followed. A lady of the parish sang a stirring acapella rendition of Psalm 42, with the congregation singing the choral response. The Gospel was read from Isaiah 25, Revelation 21, and John 14, and the minister spoke on the reality of the hope available to all in Christ. Then we had communion, after which we prayed the commendation. The service was concluded with the hymn, "Abide With Me."

The sense of presence was present throughout the service. This should not have surprised me, as the Lord himself said that where two or three are gathered in his name, there he is with us. I think the Holy Spirit was present today at St. Stephen's. Not in wild displays or explosive outbursts, but rather in a calming quietude of spirit that presided over the worship. The Gospel is real, we were assured. Christ is alive, and those who put their trust in him are assured of his grace and their own resurrection.

I myself was not unmoved by the proceedings. Assurance of grace is a recurring struggle in my spiritual life. At one point as I sat in the pew this morning, I was staring at the "service of resurrection" title printed on the bulletin. I prayed that the Lord would use the service to resurrect me from my own doubts. Later on, as I kneeled at the rail to receive communion, I prayed that Christ would take away all my doubts and sins.

It was sometime after I returned to my pew that I was struck by a simple thought. We are accustomed as Christians to confessing our faith in Jesus with the phrase, "I trust you, Lord Jesus." I confess this myself, but often I am tripped up in praying this way because I know my trust is not strong. Now I know that the strength of one's faith is irrelevant to the power of God's grace, but the phraseology still stings me. But this morning as I saw in my pew following communion, it struck me that the phrase could be reversed: "Lord Jesus, you are my trust."

A subtle shift, I know. Irrelevant and unnecessary to most believers, I'm sure. But to me, it makes all the difference – taking the emphasis off of me and putting it on Christ, where it properly and truly belongs. Confidence in myself I have none; but confidence in Christ I lack nothing. The meaning was not changed in rearranging the words – but I was. Words will not express what this really did to me; but I wager that some who have had similar experiences will understand.

There are those who say that there is no such thing as sacred space – that one can worship God as truly from a couch as from a pew. And while they have a certain point, I think they miss something. I think they miss a sense of presence. Aesthetics do not enable the grace of God. But perhaps, just perhaps,

God uses them to enable us to better receive his grace – humbling us and emphasizing to us the pre-eminence of Christ over all our smallnesses. This is a subtle thing, I know. But sometimes subtle shifts make all the difference.

April 30, 2008

ON REFLECTION: When this article was first published online, I received a wide array of responses. Some of my readers thought it was terrific – especially those who were Roman Catholic. Meanwhile, a good friend (a confirmed Protestant) accused me of wanting to be the "Scarlet Lady's flunky". Can I admit that I was equally alarmed by both sides?

On both sides, the matter revolved around the issue of "sacred space". If I was going to admit that such a thing existed, my Roman Catholic readers were only too happy to point out that they had a whole Vatican-full of other "sacred" things to share. Meanwhile, my friend was jumping up and down – warning me of the same thing!

In the midst of this, the most insightful comment I received suggested that the sense of presence which I felt came not from sacred space, but from the Holy Spirit. I think this is correct, although I confess that I yet wonder if it must be an either/or. Is it not possible that God – though he certainly *need* not, and obviously without condoning the abuses of idolatry – might sometimes choose to use aesthetics to reinforce his point?

Raining Grace

It was raining this morning in Hollidaysburg. Outside my office window – a gentle, pattering fall of water. It has stopped now, but the sidewalks are dark with moisture and the trees are sated green. At first glance, rain may not impress you: just a sort of sky-based squirt gun, writ large? But when you think about what rain really does, it's hard to be so impassive.

Rain is how the earth is watered. Water is necessary for nearly every form of organic life. Even the human body is something like 60% water. That's pretty amazing, isn't it? For every ten pieces of me, six of them are nothing but water. For babies, the percentage is even higher. Our bodies are composed of many things; but in the end, they're mostly water. Without water, we are dust.

Rain is also how the earth is transformed. Rain falls to the earth and collects into rivers. Rivers cut deep banks into the earth (witness the Grand Canyon in Arizona). Sometimes those banks are not deep enough, and the rivers flood the landscape (witness the floods in the news, or the golf course up the road from my house). Rivers flow into seas and oceans, whose waves beat an incessant cadence against the shores of every coast. In the end, rain turns even the hardest stone into sand.

I've been thinking a lot these last two days about grace. It strikes me this morning that grace is like rain. At a certain level, it falls on everybody. We all live who live, and we all breathe who have heart and lungs. In this sense, God is gracious to every living thing. He didn't have to create us, and he doesn't have to sustain us. But he does. If he did not keep it going, the universe would wink out of existence. No more warm sun, no more bright mornings and cool nights. No more smiles, no more joy: no more life.

I had an astronomy professor at university who was fond of saying, "We are of the stars." By that he meant that human life evolved from elements deposited by cosmic bombardment of the primordial Earth. But apart from the grace of God, however, even this could not be true. For just as our bodies without water are dust, so too the entire universe without God's sustaining power collapses into nothingness. Sans grace, everything is less than dust.

Grace is also like rain in that it is transforming. Rarely are we able to trace its movement – just as we are unable to entirely trace the source of the rain and the rivers. Very few Christians can tell you with complete certainty when it was that God's Spirit began to move in their lives.

But what cannot be denied is the effect of grace upon those to whom it comes. When the Holy Spirit changes a heart – when the waves of grace turn the hardened stone of a soul into a tender surf awash with faith – the change is evident. Seldom can we learn exactly when the rock became a beach; however, we cannot deny that it is sand which sticks between our toes. One of more famous twentieth century Christian authors, C.S. Lewis, described his own conversion along these very lines:

> I was driven to Whipsnade one sunny morning. When we set out I did not believe that Jesus Christ is the Son of God, and when we reached the zoo I did. Yet I had not exactly spent the journey in thought. Nor in great emotion. "Emotional" is perhaps the last word we can apply to some of the most important events. It was more like when a man, after a long sleep, still lying motionless in bed, becomes aware that he is now awake.[13]

Lewis spent the bulk of his autobiography telling the story of how he crossed from unbelief and death into spiritual life. And yet when it comes to the point – when everything finally comes clear – he can only describe it as a sort of waking up. I think that is very beautiful.

This sense of grace like rain – of grace awakening us – has been so true to my own experience. I don't have Lewis's experience of atheism in my past; so far as I can remember, I've grown up believing. However, there have been several times in my life where grace has come to me in a way that is

---

[13] C.S. Lewis, <u>Surprised by Joy</u> (New York: Harcourt Brace, 1955), p. 229

awakening – as a child, as a teen, early last year, and even this morning.

I woke up this morning fretting about grace, troubled over whether I trust Christ in the right way. I know my fretting is dung – a thing of which to be ashamed and repentant. It betrays a heart trusting in itself rather than in God; it reflects a forgetfulness about the character of grace. Salvation is not by a certain quality of faith. It is by grace through faith in the absolute quality of the Savior. Faith itself is not trusting in the quality of one's faith; it is trusting exclusively in the absolute quality of one's Savior. Yes, we exercise faith. But we are saved by grace. Period.

I have tried many things to make myself see this. I've tried praying, "repenting", and thinking about grace in the right way. I've tried getting my friends to talk sense into me. I've even tried ignoring it. Obviously all of these have been a huge success...

Why do I continue to struggle with this? Why have I been acting like a beach which wonders if it's sandy enough, or a soaked sidewalk that wonders if it's wet enough? The earth doesn't receive the rain and then water itself, nor does the rock take the breakers and pound itself into sand. The change comes only of the rain and waves. Just so with faith – it's all of grace.

This morning as I was standing in the shower it came to me what I really needed to do was just stop all this flailing. For one who confesses justification by faith alone, I have been giving a poor testimony to it. Yet I can't deny that grace has changed my heart. I can't deny that I do have faith in Christ. Perhaps it's time I just trusted him for real?

At first I tried to answer that question with a special prayer. But I ended up just laughing, and finishing (after several tries) with something like, "Okay, Jesus." The point was taken. I sure hope it sticks. Grace is not a self-help kit. Grace is like the rain. And it *is* raining.

May 16, 2008

RUSTLING LEAVES

When I was in junior and senior high school, the bus stop was about a half mile from my house. In the mornings it was either a downhill walk or a quick ride from my Dad. On the afternoons when my parents worked, however, it was an uphill walk. The bus would come to a hissing stop and the door would clank open. Down the steps and out the door we would dutifully trudge – out the door and up the hill.

Besides myself, the long walk was shared by a handful of other kids who lived up the hill. Sometimes we would walk together, sometimes not – depending on the weather and our relative moods. Speaking of weather, it really could vary. Fall was the best: crisp air, colored foliage, with either a mild sun or benign clouds hung in the clear sky. Winter was the worst, of course. And somewhere in the middle we had Spring.

Seriously: Spring could go either way. Sometimes it was much like Fall. Other times, it rained. (It is this schizophrenia that keeps it second-rated to Fall in my order-loving Presbyterian sensibilities.) It was on one of the latter occasions when I noticed something peculiar about the leaves.

Truth be told, it was not I who noticed it. Rather, it was one of the other kids on the walk home – an older boy who always walked on the wrong side of the road but who seemed to think *I* was the one walking on the wrong side! (I mean, *honestly!*) Anyway, it was this older boy who pointed out to me something which I have never forgotten: that the leaves on trees tend to lift up toward the sky just before it rains — almost as if they could sense that it was coming.

As I was preparing to write this afternoon, it was beginning to raining. Once again, the leaves were upturned. I did a web search to see what I could learn, and found some stuff about shifts in wind vectors and variances in air pressure. This is probably on track, so far as it goes. Nevertheless, to the (mostly) uninformed observer like myself it still seems as though the leaves act out of a sort of prescience — an *expectation*.

In the positive sense, expectation is closely tied to hope. In fact, the Greek word *elpis* denotes both concepts. Hope is one of the most fundamental human needs. I don't think we tend to think of it as such consciously; after all, it is not nearly as immediate to our minds as the more tangible needs for water, food, shelter, and clothing. Depending on the amount of fat in our bodies and other physical characteristics, we may survive up to a week without water or a month without food. Depending on the weather, we may survive outdoors for a matter of weeks or months. And according to some experiments, we may survive several years with insufficient clothing (you can see these experiments in-progress at your local shopping mall).

But how long can we survive without hope? I'm not talking about a bad day here, or even a bad week. I'm talking about a state of existence in which we suffer ultimate despair. Could we survive even an hour? Is this not what we see in the last words of so many tragic suicides – a seeming complete lack of hope?

What does real hope look like? Unfortunately, our vision today is fogged by a lot of nonsense. Our world is full of would-be sources of hope. There are careers, family aspirations, fame, and success. There are health and fitness regimes, political campaigns, and false religions. Sometimes the line between these latter two can get blurry – on both the Left and the Right. Sometimes any one or more of these false sources of hope dress themselves up in Christian clothing and come to church. Sometimes – God help us – they even come out of the churches.

How can we tell the difference, then, between false and real hope? The answer is actually simpler than you might think. The delineation between false and real hope comes down to something inherent in the former. What do I mean? What I'm talking about here is that sense of *uncertainty* which one always finds in false sources of hope. *Is this really going to satisfy me? Is this what life is really about? Will this not only carry me through life, but beyond death? Is there life beyond death? If so, have I done enough to earn it?* Even false religions are not immune to this uncertainty – though they do their damnedest (literally) to cover it up with a lot of religious claptrap.

The hallmark of every false hope is that it is *anthropocentric*. That is, it centers itself upon the actions and efforts and motives of humankind. You can hear it expressed in such slogans as, "Believe in yourself," "God helps those who help themselves," "Pull yourself up by your bootstraps," or even, "Become a better you." If one is to be satisfied in life; if one is to know what life is all about; if there is an afterlife – then it falls to one to obtain these things by one's own efforts. *Carpe diem*, says false hope, "You can do it."

Trouble is, we know damned well (again, literally) that this is a lie. We are each of us thoroughly wicked in thought, word, and deed. And though we may not quite understand how, we each intrinsically sense that our own wickedness undercuts any chance of finding security in ourselves. Oh, some of us are better at suppressing this truth than others. It's like grilling a steak, really. The cuts produced by the butcher may vary, but keep applying the heat and you will sear even the thickest cut – eventually charring it all the way through.[14] So we may each vary in our individual levels of truth-suppression. None of us, however, are completely able to obliterate our sense of uncertainty about our false hopes. The meekest worldling or the darkest tyrant may sleep easy some nights; but nobody sleeps easy every night. The proof

---

[14] See Romans 1:18-32

is all around us – from the tall stacks of liquor in the pubs to the shiny stacks of pills at the pharmacy.

Nor, likewise, are any of us able to completely ignore that whisper echoing deep within us that *it ought not be so*. Despite a seemingly endless raft of evidence to the contrary – wars, famines, institutionalized injustice, and death – we cannot help but believe things were *meant* to be different. Moreover, we cannot help but believe – even if it is a faint, faltering belief – that someday, some way, things *will* be different. In short, we are rather like addicts: we find in ourselves a desire which we are both unable to fill and unable to do without. We are hopeless; nevertheless, we hope.

Faced with such a startling contradiction, we must accept one of two possibilities. The first is that there really is no such thing as lasting, real hope; and that all our flailing to the contrary is nothing but pitiable Pollyanna lowing. If this is the case, then we really are like those who suffer from a chemical addiction – and the only solution therefore is a process of slow, painful exorcism. If we are truly hopeless, then we must learn to stop hoping. But this 'cure' may prove more painful than the disease; for, as mentioned earlier, can we really continue to exist in a state of despair?

The other possibility is that all our yearnings are not simply a cruel joke of our nature; that real hope does exist. Yet we know instinctively that this hope cannot come from us. Where, then, can we find it?

The message of Christianity – the message of the Bible – is that real hope does exist, yet can only come from outside ourselves, from God himself. All of Scripture – from Abraham in Genesis, to the prophets of the Israelite kingdom, through the Lord Jesus in the Gospels, to the epistles and finally to John's Revelation – bear witness to this constant theme: that the hope we cannot obtain on our own, God has provided for us. As the prophet Jonah put it (from within the belly of a whale): "Salvation belongs to the LORD!"[15]

Out of his grace, God has provided a way to mend our broken race. His justice must punish sin – so his love has provided a substitute sin-bearer. His law requires perfect obedience – so his mercy has provided one to obey perfectly. This one person – the only one upon whom all real hope must center – is Jesus Christ. He was perfect in life and thus immortal by right, yet died for sinners. In his death he bore the curse and wrath due to sin, and three days later rose to everlasting life and victory. For those who receive him, there is real hope. Hope that, just as we are joined to him in his death to sin, so we shall be united to him in his resurrection.[16] Hope that nothing can separate us from his love[17], and that in the end, death itself will be vanquished.[18]

---

[15] Jonah 2:9
[16] Romans 6:5
[17] Romans 8:31-38
[18] 1 Corinthians 15:26

But how are we to receive him? How can we who are innately hopeless obtain such hope? Here again, we do well to consider the leaves. They do not ascend the skies to grasp the rain; rather, they simply turn themselves toward it. Receiving Christ is the same way. No level of human effort – be it good works or perfect piety – can ever earn his grace. The only way to receive Jesus is to abandon oneself to him. All thoughts of self-salvation, all trusting in false hopes, must be cast aside as rubbish. We must give up on ourselves completely; we must give ourselves up to him totally. Simply put, we must trust him alone to save us.[19] Here – and here only – is where real hope begins.

But what exactly is it that Christians hope for? And what makes our hope any more certain – any less false – than all the other hopes being peddled on a thousand corners, ten thousand television commercials, one hundred thousand billboards, and a million websites?

To answer the former question, I can do no better than to quote the very passage which has inspired the title of this essay:

> … the poets tell us such lovely falsehoods. They talk as if the west wind could really sweep into a human soul; but it can't. They tell us that "beauty born of murmuring sound" will pass

---

[19] Romans 4:1-5

into a human face; but it won't. Or not yet. For if we take the imagery of Scripture seriously, if we believe that God will one day *give* us the Morning Star and cause us to *put on* the splendour of the sun, then we may surmise that both the ancient myths and the modern poetry, so false as history, may be very near the truth as prophecy. At present we are on the outside of the world, the wrong side of the door. We discern the freshness and purity of morning, but they do not make us fresh and pure. We cannot mingle with the splendours we see. But all the leaves of the New Testament are rustling with the rumour that it will not always be so. Some day, God willing, we shall get *in*... Nature is mortal; we shall outlive her. When all the suns and nebulae have passed away, each one of you will still be alive. Nature is only the image, the symbol; but it is the symbol which Scripture invites me to use. We are summoned to pass in through Nature, beyond her, into that splendour which she fitfully reflects. And there, in beyond Nature, we shall eat of the tree of life.[20]

As we can see, the Christian hope is scarcely expressible: to delineate its parts is to stretch human language nearly to the breaking. Full consummation of

---

[20] C.S. Lewis, <u>The Weight of Glory: and Other Addresses</u> (New York: HarperCollins, 2001), pp. 43-44.

our communion with God and creation; fresh apprehension of the glory of God through the fellowship of his Son; forgiveness, immortality, restoration. In short: life, *as we all know it was meant to be*. But what makes this hope any more certain that all the rest?

The answer, dear friends, is found in the name – the certainty of Christian hope is found in Christ himself. Just as salvation itself comes from outside ourselves, so also its certainty. Christian hope is based not on the character or accomplishments of its believers, but solely on the accomplishment and character of Jesus Christ. To put it alliteratively: God is the guarantee.

It is difficult to overstate the difference that this makes. If Christian hope were based in any part on human efforts, then it would be no more certain than the myriad false hopes in our modern Vanity Fair. "But what of faith and good works?" you will ask. Are these not necessary?

Yes, good works must flow from Christian faith[21]; but they are the house, never the foundation.[22] Yes, faith is necessary; one cannot be saved apart from faith in Christ. Yet even at this simplest level of faith, human effort cannot be a grounds of hope: for if it is up to us to have a certain "threshold" level or quality of faith in order to be saved, faith becomes just another work to earn God's love – because,

---

[21] James 2:17
[22] Romans 4:2

apparently, Christ did not do enough on his own to secure it. And more to the point (as if that last thought were not bad enough), we are left wondering: *have I believed enough?*[23] Yes, some knowledge is required of the rational Christian: what is sin? who is Christ? Nevertheless, a Christian is most characterized not by *what* he knows or *how well* he knows it, but by *who* he knows — or to put it more biblically, by *whom* he is known. Faith is therefore the instrument of salvation, but never its basis.[24] Perfect understanding is not required, nor perfect faith — only a sinner trusting in a perfect Savior.

Against all anthropocentrism, then — against all false hopes — stands the Christian hope of salvation by grace alone, through faith alone, in Christ alone. Hope isn't found in the mirror, but in the Maker. If we would but be like the upturned leaves — turning our eyes away from earth, away from ourselves; turning our whole selves upward toward his merciful raining grace — then we will have real, certain hope. And not only have it, friends — we will be positively rustling with it.

June 28, 2008

---

[23] See Timothy Keller, The Reason for God: Belief in an Age of Skepticism (New York: Penguin, 2008), p. 234. Or just flip back in this book to p. 41, where I have quoted the relevant passage.
[24] WCF 11.1-2

DISCONNECTED & DOWNCAST

One of the most horrible feelings you can experience in this life is disconnection. Those of you who have experienced it will know what I'm talking about. Disconnection: that sense of utter, unbridgeable distance and separation from the things or persons whom you love. It is like a chalice of uncertainty, or a horn-full of the mead of helplessness.

About two years ago, I was in Redlands, California on a Thursday afternoon when my cell phone rang. It was my wife. She was eight months pregnant, and had just been to her OB-GYN appointment, for one of the regular weekly check-ups. When I asked her how the appointment went, she did not mince words: she was having sharp pains in her back; the doctor said she was several centimeters dilated; they expected she would give birth within a day or two. Oh, and could I come home today, please?

There is a unique sense of terror one experiences upon suddenly learning that one is three thousand miles away from the imminent birth of one's child. Add the fact that said imminent birth is coming a month premature, and you descend to new places of panic. Could I come home today? Could I? Woe betide those who would stand in my way!

There was just one problem: it was the Thursday prior to Independence Day weekend. In other words, all the flights – all over the country – were booked and overbooked. Several frantic conversations with the company travel department later, I was left with mixed news and more uncertainty. They could get me to Phoenix on Thursday, but could not guarantee getting me back to Pittsburgh. I could try getting on the standby lists; but if that didn't pan out, I'd be stuck in Phoenix until the date of my original return flight to the East Coast – Friday afternoon.

Well, what could I do? A gracious coworker drove me back to my hotel (I had walked to the office that day), where I packed up and egressed as quickly as I could to make the flight for Phoenix. Arriving in Phoenix, I tried everything I could – but the two flights to Pittsburgh were full. It seems I was stuck in Phoenix until Friday afternoon after all. I tell you: *that* was not a pleasant phone call to make.

It was not a pleasant experience in any respect. In order to find dinner, I had to leave the secure area. Not wanting to risk missing a cab or any other peril common to extreme travel, I was unwilling to risk leaving the airport for an offsite hotel. Thus I spent a night in the terminal, sleeping fitfully on a chair while clutching my bags. I bought Walter Isaacson's biography of Benjamin Franklin (an interesting book, by the way) to help pass time. But under the circumstances, one could only read so much. One could only sleep so much, too – what with the announcement, every five minutes, that – surprise! – firearms were not permitted in the airport terminal. Thank you, TSA.

After a morning passed fretting away in the Phoenix airport on minimal sleep, I boarded a plane at 3 PM to Pittsburgh. Landing late at 10:30 PM (a flight made to feel even longer by the teenage girls sitting next to me on the plane, one of whom played Nirvana on her laptop, and the other of whom was a mother herself), I ran through the terminal and got out of the airport by 11 PM. There was a voicemail on my phone: had I landed yet? How far was I from the hospital? My wife was in labor at this point, but they were going to try to slow things down.

The drive back to Johnstown was another adventure. You want to know why I eschew tail-gating people on the highway? Because I was tail-gated that night by some punk. Looking in the mirror, I remember muttering something dark about, "If looks were cruise missiles, kid..." You want to know why I like motorcycles? Because providentially, I subsequently got behind a motorcyclist whose penchant for speed allowed me to follow him a significant portion of the way home from a radar-safe distance – well in excess of the legal limit.

That is, until we ran into the State Police sobriety check-point. (No, I'm not making this up.) Cycle Boy got pulled in, I was waived through. Thank you, Cycle Boy. And thank you, God. Despite the fear of delay, even this turned to my advantage. Feeling secure in the knowledge that most of the officers in the vicinity were now behind me, I was able to make very good time the rest of the way to Johnstown.

As it turns out, I did make it home on time for the birth of my second son. Only just, however. I arrived at the hospital at 12:30 AM. My son was born at 1:34 AM.

Throughout this harrowing journey – and for the entirety of the nine days after his birth during which my son was kept in the hospital's Natal Intensive Care Unit with under-developed lungs – I went through some of the most extreme feelings of helplessness that I have ever experienced. The impotence one feels in such circumstances is, well, potent. You feel almost as though you are floating through your days, seeing everything through a fog. Fireworks that weekend? Who cares. Rather like a balloon that's lost its tether, you drift from worry to prayer to sleep to weeping – and back again.

My second son celebrated his second birthday this past week. By God's grace, he's a healthy, strapping, dirt-eating boy. This weekend, I am going to preach a sermon on Psalm 42. Interestingly enough, the theme of that text is hope: hope for those who feel disconnected from God; hope for those whose feelings of disconnection lead them into a certain downcastedness of soul.

The Psalmist in Psalm 42 (though not explicitly mentioned, identified by some as David before he was king) has been cut off from the tabernacle in Jerusalem. His trust in God remains, but having been cut off from the outward means of God's grace – the sacrifices, the altar, etc. – he feels disconnected. In the absence of the faith-fortifying ceremonies and worship of the tabernacle, the stress of his exile is starting to gnaw at his faith. Unable to feed his soul its "vitamins," he is hearing ever more loudly the taunts of the world, the flesh, and the devil. And he's feeling ever more keenly the burden of difficult providences — he compares them to roaring waterfalls, waves, and breakers. And like a man caught beneath the waves, he feels the tug of the deep. Like a cancer in his bones, the abyss calls to his spirit: "Despair! God hath forgotten thee!"

And yet in all this, the Psalmist maintains hope. When circumstances prevent him feeling the presence of God outwardly — when words of explanation fail — he centers his hope on God. Turning his eyes outward, he lifts them to, "the God of my life" (v. 8), whose love watches over him during the day like a command, and is with him like a song in the night. When he is hopelessly downcast in himself, he hopes in God:

Why are you cast down, O my soul,
and why are you in turmoil within me?
Hope in God; for I shall again praise him,
my salvation and my God. [25]

The day that I first read that verse, I wept — for I myself was feeling downcast and disconnected from God. As I prepared the sermon this week, however, it

---

[25] Psalm 42:5-6a, 11

struck me that as Christians, we need never despair that we are disconnected from God. We have access to God from any place. Jesus himself says that we need not go to Jerusalem, but only worship in spirit and in truth.[26] And Jesus Christ himself is that Truth.[27] Though absent from us now in body, he gives us his Holy Spirit to cheer and to guide us.[28]

Why do we still find ourselves downcast, then? I think perhaps it's because we forget this aspect of the Gospel – that God is always with those who trust him. He is never far from us. Or perhaps we distance ourselves by willful sins – such as neglecting the means of grace. If we neglect to be at prayer or in the Word, are we surprised that God seems distant?[29] Or if we absent ourselves in mind and/or in body from the public worship where he promises to meet us, are we surprised that we can't sense his presence?[30] Or, most often, perhaps we just believe the lies – forgetting that nothing can separate Christians from the love of God in Christ Jesus our Lord.[31]

Disconnection makes us acutely downcast. And though it be true that, sometimes, providence requires separation from earthly loves, it is never – never – the case that those who trust Christ as God and Savior are separated from his love or presence. If we have

---

[26] See John 4:19-26
[27] John 14:6
[28] John 14:17
[29] John 17:17
[30] Matthew 18:20
[31] See Romans 8:38-39

committed ourselves to his glorious grace, we know that we will not thirst forever.

"Why are you downcast, O my soul? And why are you in turmoil within me?" Hope in Christ; for I *shall* again praise him, my salvation and my God.

July 5, 2008

A PARABLE OF GRACE & CHOCOLATE

Robert was a Christian young man in turmoil. To all outward appearances, there was nothing wrong: he had a steady job, was faithful to his church, and took constant thought to his obligation to love God and neighbor. He read his Bible and prayed seriously, and he was diligent to attend and participate in his church's public worship. He supported his church community in whatever way he could: he gave regular offerings, he helped with maintenance of the church grounds, and he was generous in his friendships.

And yet, as I said, Robert was in turmoil. He had not always been so outwardly upstanding. He had done some things during his youth of which he was now most ashamed. One portion of his history in particular had been eating away at him. Try as he might, he couldn't seem to stop thinking about it. So one day, he did what you might expect: he made an appointment to see his minister.

Pastor John was already waiting when he arrived at the coffee shop. After ordering a mocha, Robert joined him at a small, nicely-private table near the back corner of the shop.

"Thank you for seeing me on such short notice, Pastor."

"No problem, Bob. What's going on?"

"Well, I have a problem. It's hard for me to talk about."

"That's okay, Bob. Take your time."

73

"It's kinda embarrassing..."

"We're all sinners, son. Tell me what's on your mind." Fully expecting that Bob's trouble had to do with some of the more conventional struggles of young single men, the Reverend John was unprepared for what came next.

"Well, it's right here in front of me." Bob pointed to his coffee.

"You have a problem with coffee?"

"No, not coffee, Pastor. This is a mocha; my problem is with chocolate."

"Oh?" John was not sure what to make of this revelation. Bob was not an overweight guy. Did he have some sort of secret addiction that he covered up with exercise or anorexia?

"Yes. You see, I love chocolate. But every time I eat it, I fear I might be living in unrepentant sin."

Pastor John was now genuinely puzzled. "Go on, son."

"Ok. Quite a few years ago – when I was a teenager – I got caught trying to shoplift a chocolate bar from a grocery store."

"You got caught? I don't remember hearing about this from your parents." Bob's parents had been members of John's church since Bob had been a boy.

"Well, Dad and Mom never found out. You see, I got caught in the act by the store clerk – but managed to get away before he could grab me."

"I see. Did you ask God to forgive you for stealing?"

"Yes, but that's not the issue."

"Oh. Go on, then."

Bob frowned. "Even after I had escaped that day, I was terrified that I was going to get caught. Even after I had made it back to my house, I squirmed every time I saw a police car – sure that they were going to come and arrest me. And so I made a vow."

"A vow?"

"Yes. I prayed to God and vowed that if he would keep me from getting caught, I would never eat chocolate again."

"Um."

"For awhile, I was faithful. For a few months, at least. But some time later, I disregarded the vow under the reasoning (or perhaps the rationalization) that God doesn't make deals like the one I asked him to make. But I could never really be sure, see? I asked a good friend what I should do about a broken vow – without giving him all the details, obviously. He said that I should simply repent of making the vow and ask forgiveness."

John nodded. "And did you?"

"Yes, right away. But the problem is, I can't find anywhere in the Bible where this happens – where a person can repent of a vow to God and not be bound anymore."

"Ok."

"What should I do, Pastor? This has been eating at me for a long time." Bob's tone was obviously pained, and his voice picked up speed as the words tumbled out of him. "I realize it's pretty stupid to think that something which happened so many years back could still matter. But every time I read in the Bible about 'paying vows' to God, I wince. I hope my friend was right – because I really don't want to have to live the rest of my life without chocolate. But I also don't want to go to Hell. I'll give up chocolate if I have to. But do I? Something just doesn't smell right about the whole thing."

Pastor John leaned back in his chair, his expression unreadable. His eyes fell to peer down at his coffee mug, squinting. Bob felt himself growing anxious. What was he thinking? After what must have only been a few moments – but which seemed like an hour to Bob – Pastor John glanced up.

"So," he began grimly, focusing from beneath his eyebrows, "you asked God to become an accessory after the fact to a crime."

Bob's jaw dropped open. John could see in his eyes that the wheels were spinning, but sensed the boy needed a bit more to gain traction.

"You asked God to drive the getaway car. That's asking God to commit sin, son. Read Psalm 50. You thought God was like you, and would go along with your scheme to avoid capture."

"What?"

"You asked him to help you avoid lawful authority – lawful authority which Romans 13 and 1 Peter 2 tell us he ordains."

"I hadn't thought of that."

"The vow you made was not to the God of Scripture, son – but to a god of your own making."

"I don't understand."

John took a deep breath. "A vow is an act of worship, Bob."

"Yes, I've read that. I've read a lot about vows recently."

"Good, then perhaps you've also read what the Catechism has to say about worship. Specifically, think of the second commandment. What does it forbid?"

Bob's answer was instant. "The worship of idols."

"Yes," said John, "but that's not all. The Catechism not only forbids the making or worshipping of idols of false deities; it also forbids the worship of God by images."

"I don't see where you're going, Pastor. I wasn't thinking of any picture when I made my vow. I was just praying to God."

"No you weren't," John replied, then went on before Bob could respond. "Think of what the Israelites did at Sinai while Moses was on the mountain. What happened when Moses took longer to return than they expected?"

Again, Bob's response came too quick. "They made a golden calf, and worshipped it."

"That's not all. You're missing something critical."

"You mean the-" Bob hesitated, clearly puzzled, "-the orgy?"

"No, Bob," John said firmly. "Focus your mind. They were not worshipping just a calf. They were idolaters, to be sure – but it's not as simple as that. They were worshipping God through the image of the calf – or so they thought."

"You mean that when they were sacrificing to the idol, they thought they were sacrificing to God?"

"Exactly. If you look at Exodus 32, you'll see it in the text. When Aaron sees the calf, he builds an altar and proclaims a feast – 'to the LORD.'"

"Wow," Bob said quietly, "I never thought of that passage like that."

John had to smother his annoyance. Hadn't he given all the graduates a copy of Packer's *Knowing God*? Recovering himself quickly, he went on. "You should think about it, son. Think about it hard – because you are in the same boat as they."

Bob looked bewildered. "I'm not arguing, Pastor, but I don't see how."

"When you made your vow, did you have in mind the God of Scripture, or somebody else?"

"I thought it was the God of Scripture."

"What you thought is immaterial, son. The Israelites thought they were worshipping God, too. But God condemned them for idolatry for attempting to worship him via a false image."

"But I didn't mean anything like that, Pastor. I just knew that God was merciful, and was asking for mercy."

"Yes, but an incomplete image is also false. And your image was incomplete, Bob, because it left off God's holiness — a holiness which would never allow him to be an accessory to your criminal behavior."

"Oh." Bob looked genuinely shocked. "Even though I didn't think so at the time, I suppose I made my vow not to God," — he looked up — "but to an image of him I had constructed."

"A false image," John corrected, "A god you made in your own image."

For a minute, Bob didn't say a word. When he spoke again, his voice carried an appropriately sober inflection. "That means I was — am — an idolater."

"Yes."

"And so it is the vow itself that must be repented of?" he ventured tentatively.

"Yes."

"Because it was false?"

"It is a false vow because you made it to someone who isn't God, and you asked for something that was against the revealed nature and will of the true and living God."

"Oh." Bob bowed his head for a minute, praying silently. John took a long drink of his coffee, smiling kindly. Idolatry was no laughing matter; but repentance was always a cause for rejoicing. When Bob raised his head again, his expression was still troubled.

"Well, I asked the Lord to forgive me. And I believe he has."

"But?"

"But Pastor, I have to be frank with you. I don't feel better. In fact, I feel horrible and ashamed – because I'm more relieved that I can go on eating chocolate than I am grieved over my sin. Can I even call myself a Christian, being this wretched?"

Pastor John's smile was sympathetic. "Wretched?" he said, "Welcome to Pauline religion."

"But why don't I feel worse about what I've done?"

"Is it your feelings that make you forgiven, or the work of Christ alone?"

"The latter," Bob said embarrassedly. "But maybe if I gave up chocolate now – to show God how sorry I am – I'd feel better?"

The smile faded, and the brows closed. "Are you asking me if you should do penance, son?"

Bob's face fell. "Am I?"

"Penance may be psychologically satisfying, but it's theologically worthless."

July 9, 2008

The Empty Bench

A few blocks away from my home in Hollidaysburg stands the husk of the once-mighty Highland Hall — an expansive stone building with several wings, several porticos, and myriad windows situated atop a green mound. On one side of the Hall is a small friary; but mostly, it is surrounded by a well-treed, wonderfully undeveloped park. In all, the Highland Hall "campus" spreads over an entire block near the center of town. Surrounded on two sides by a stone wall, and one other by a hedgerow, it is a splendid place to let my children wander off some energy as they explore such mysteries as the "Monster Cave": a hole in the bole of an old gnarled tree on the hillside which must — by necessity! — be the dwelling and hearth-home of some nefarious beast.

When I think about Highland Hall, several questions come to mind. Were the stones of its walls taken from the nearby Juniata River? How long, and how many men, did it take to build? How many lives have passed through its portals — how many souls have trod its now-empty passages? On the back side of Highland Hall, there is a yard. Along the north edge of this yard sits an old, weather-worn bench — its planks bowed by the many seasons and seats it has seen. I love to sit on this bench. It is a fine place to read, to pray, or simply to ponder. It is one of those places that feels simultaneously habitable and haunted.

It is this latter, haunted quality that intrigues me so. I find the same quality in empty landscapes, or in lonesome paths through orange woods in the Fall. Clearly such locales bear the footprints of Twilight – that long, inexorable march towards decline that is the way of all flesh; the entropic slide which plagues all of creation. In this sense, it is remarkable to me that I find such places so appealing. I have never been a great fan of horror films or novels. Why then – especially as a Christian – am I so fascinated with what seems, at first blush, to be the places of this world that hint most strongly of the macabre?

As I sit and ruminate over these questions, a verse from the book of Ecclesiastes comes to mind. As a young man, the book of Ecclesiastes was my favorite book of Scripture – to the point that I once read the entire thing in one sitting. The verse I have in mind is the fifteenth verse of the first chapter: "What is crooked cannot be made straight, and what is lacking cannot be counted." What is lacking cannot be counted. I have been struck by that phrase from the first time I considered it. It seems to explain – or at least intimate an explanation – of my experience.

It is like a dirge sung over the enormity of what has been lost to the ravages of history and human mortality, a deep sighing over the seeming futility of life in a world where so much is gone before it can fully bloom. How many bones lie buried beneath our feet, of which we remain completely ignorant? How many untold generations – how many millions, how many billions of souls — have passed through the world without so much as "a memory of light"[32] to bear them witness?

I confess that, had I no hope, I would want to end it all. Why continue to play along, if it all be naught but a charade? If there really is no glimmer of dawn at the end of the dark night, what is the point of waiting for nightfall — why not make the terminus on one's own terms?

And yet I am not without hope. For alongside of that vespers verse from Ecclesiastes, there rings in my mind its morningtide corollary: "What no eye has seen, nor ear heard, nor the heart of man imagined, what God has prepared for those who love him."[33] The import of these words changes everything.

The Christian hope is that the approaching Twilight is not merely the forward march of a cold, empty, and everlasting night. The sun may bloat and die; the stars may fall; but not into a bottomless cauldron of inert Void. The Christian hope is that approaching Twilight is the herald of the great and magnificent Morning to follow — where all the moons of mourning shall be chased away by the glorious Saving Son of God!

It for this reason that I find solace in walking those empty Autumn paths through pumpkin-colored woods. It is in this hope that I continue to visit the

---

[32] I borrow this phrase from the title of Robert Jordan's final *Wheel of Time* novel, which itself will be published posthumously.
[33] 1 Corinthians 2:9

forgotten yard at Highland Hall. The seemingly inevitable slide into entropy was overturned in a moment when Jesus Christ rose from dead. By grace through faith in him, I have hope. Hope that just as I have been united to him in his death, so shall I be united with him in his resurrection.[34] And so the haunted quality of lonely places is forever changed from a whisper of despair into a zephyr of delight. For twilight is no longer simply the last, lingering glimpse before nightfall; it has become the bracing, final blink before morning. As Scripture puts it so potently: "The last enemy to be destroyed is death."[35]

Jesus is coming. The empty bench will not be empty forever.

July 12, 2008

---

[34] Romans 6:5
[35] 1 Corinthians 15:26

ABOUT THE AUTHOR

Jeremiah W. Montgomery graduated from the University of Pittsburgh with a B.S. in Computer Science and minors in Mathematics and Philosophy. He is currently the Pastoral Assistant at Westminster Church (Orthodox Presbyterian) in Hollidaysburg, Pennsylvania, and a student at Greenville Presbyterian Theological Seminary.

He is the author of numerous articles and reviews available at his blog, *The Far Green Country*. He is the author of *Soulmancer*, a novel of epic fantasy, and *Making Tea*, a collection of essays.

He and his family reside in Hollidaysburg, Pennsylvania.

WWW.PIPEANDPINT.COM
WWW.PIPEANDPINT.COM/BLOG

www.ingramcontent.com/pod-product-compliance
Lightning Source LLC
Chambersburg PA
CBHW030112070426
42448CB00036B/688